JR. GRAPHIC AMERICAN INVENTORS

# ELI WHITNEY

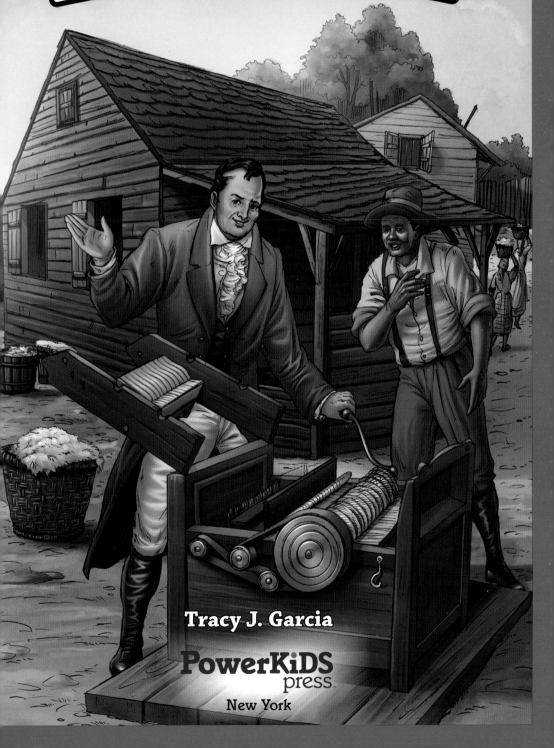

Tracy J. Garcia

## PowerKiDS press

New York

Published in 2013 by The Rosen Publishing Group, Inc.
29 East 21st Street, New York, NY 10010

First Edition

Editor: Joanne Randolph

Book Design: Planman Technologies

Illustrations: Planman Technologies


**Library of Congress Cataloging-in-Publication Data**

Garcia, Tracy J.

Eli Whitney / by Tracy J. Garcia. — 1st ed.

  p. cm. — (Jr. graphic American inventors)

Includes index.

ISBN 978-1-4777-0075-4 (library binding) — ISBN 978-1-4777-0135-5 (pbk.)
— ISBN 978-1-4777-0136-2 (6-pack)

1. Whitney, Eli, 1765-1825—Juvenile literature.
2. Inventors—United States—Biography—Juvenile literature.
3. Cotton gins and ginning—Juvenile literature. I. Title.

TS1570.W4G37 2013

609.2—dc23

[B]

2012019319


Manufactured in the United States of America

CPSIA Compliance Information: Batch #W13PK1: For Further Information contact Rosen
Publishing, New York, New York at 1-800-237-9932

# Contents

# Introduction

Eli Whitney was an inventor and a pioneer of modern **manufacturing**. He is widely known as the inventor of the **cotton gin**, a machine that transformed the US **economy** before the **Civil War**. The **factory system** he helped develop allowed work to be done faster and better.

# Main Characters

**Catharine Greene Miller** (1755–1814) Widow of General Nathanael Greene, hero of the **American Revolution**. She owned the cotton **plantation** Miller and Whitney worked on. Married Phineas Miller in 1796.

**Phineas Miller** (1764–1803) Yale graduate and manager of Catharine Greene's plantation in Georgia. Helped Whitney create the cotton gin. Married Catharine Greene in 1796.

**Eli Whitney** (1765–1825) Famous inventor best known for inventing the cotton gin. He also popularized the idea of **assembly-line** manufacturing and **interchangeable parts**, which are both used today in modern industry.

**Eli Whitney Jr.** (1820–?) Only son of Eli Whitney. Took over his father's armory in 1841.

**Henrietta Edwards Whitney** (1786–1870) Daughter of a well-respected New England family. Married Eli Whitney in 1817.

# ELI WHITNEY

AS A CHILD, ELI WHITNEY LIVED ON A FARM IN WESTBOROUGH, MASSACHUSETTS.

Manchester •

**Boston** •
★ Westborough

Springfield •
Providence •

• Newport

ELI LIKED TO EXPERIMENT IN HIS FATHER'S WORKSHOP.

I HAD BETTER GET MY FATHER'S WATCH BACK TOGETHER BEFORE HE GETS HOME. MAYBE I SHOULD NOT HAVE TAKEN IT APART.

DURING THE AMERICAN REVOLUTION, ELI SAW AN OPPORTUNITY TO USE HIS TALENT. SINCE THERE WAS A GREAT NEED FOR NAILS, HE WOULD MAKE THEM IN HIS FATHER'S SHOP.

I CAN SELL THESE NAILS TO THE FARMERS, MERCHANTS, AND CRAFTSMEN AROUND TOWN.

ELI'S MOTHER HAD DIED WHEN HE WAS A CHILD. HIS STEPMOTHER THOUGHT HE SHOULD SPEND MORE TIME WORKING ON THE FARM AND LESS TIME IN THE SHOP.

I SEE YOU BROKE ONE OF YOUR KNIVES. I CAN FIX IT IN THE SHOP.

ELI, HOW WILL YOU DO THAT? THESE ARE THE FINEST KNIVES FROM ENGLAND!

JUST GIVE ME A CHANCE.

ELI FIXED HIS STEPMOTHER'S KNIFE SO IT LOOKED LIKE NEW.

SEE, I DID IT!

ELI, YOUR WORK IS REMARKABLE!

IN 1785, WHITNEY ENROLLED AT LEICESTER ACADEMY, A PRIVATE SCHOOL IN LEICESTER, MASSACHUSETTS, TO PREPARE FOR COLLEGE. HE WOULD STUDY GREEK, LATIN, SCRIPTURE, AND MATHEMATICS.

WHITNEY ENTERED YALE COLLEGE, IN NEW HAVEN, CONNECTICUT, IN 1789.

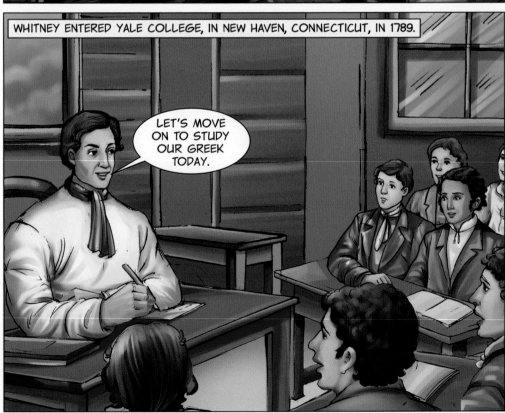

WHEN HE GRADUATED, WHITNEY WAS IN DEBT AND NEEDED A JOB. HE MET WITH THE PRESIDENT OF THE COLLEGE, EZRA STILES.

MR. WHITNEY, YOU HAVE BEEN A FINE STUDENT. I CAN HELP YOU GET A JOB AS A TUTOR, BUT YOU MUST MOVE TO THE SOUTH.

YES, SIR!

MR. PHINEAS MILLER, ANOTHER YALE GRADUATE, WILL HELP WITH INTRODUCTIONS.

WHITNEY GOT A JOB AS A TUTOR ON A PLANTATION IN SOUTH CAROLINA. BEFORE REPORTING TO HIS TUTORING JOB, HE WOULD VISIT PHINEAS MILLER IN GEORGIA.

Atlanta

Georgia

Savannah

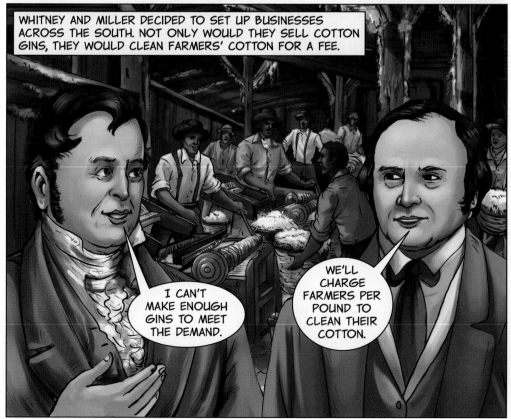

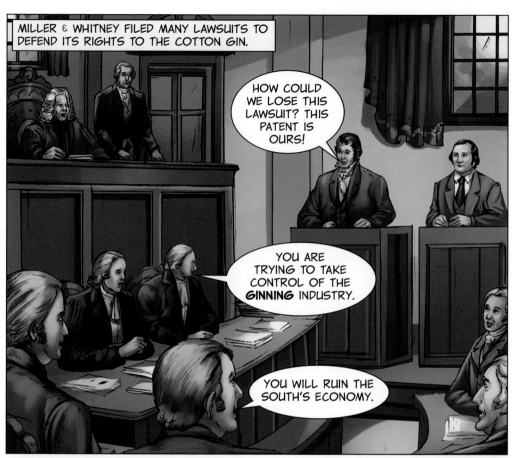

MILLER & WHITNEY FILED MANY LAWSUITS TO DEFEND ITS RIGHTS TO THE COTTON GIN.

HOW COULD WE LOSE THIS LAWSUIT? THIS PATENT IS OURS!

YOU ARE TRYING TO TAKE CONTROL OF THE **GINNING** INDUSTRY.

YOU WILL RUIN THE SOUTH'S ECONOMY.

IT TOOK YEARS OF LAWSUITS BEFORE MILLER & WHITNEY WOULD BE PAID FOR ITS INVENTION.

I AM TIRED OF ALL THESE LAWSUITS. I NEED A DIFFERENT PROJECT!

THE COTTON GIN INCREASED THE DEMAND FOR COTTON. SOUTHERN PLANTERS NEEDED MORE ENSLAVED PEOPLE TO WORK THE FIELDS.

THE COTTON GIN CHANGED THE ECONOMY. **TEXTILE MILLS** OPENED ALL OVER NEW ENGLAND PROVIDING THOUSANDS OF JOBS MAKING COTTON CLOTH.

SINCE THE COTTON GIN ALLOWED WORKERS TO PRODUCE MORE COTTON, THE PRICE OF COTTON CLOTH FELL. CLOTHES BECAME MORE AFFORDABLE.

I CAN BUY MORE CLOTHES FOR THE CHILDREN.

I CAN AFFORD NICE COTTON DRESSES.

WHITNEY WENT TO WASHINGTON, D.C., LOOKING FOR AN OPPORTUNITY. HE MET WITH HIS FRIEND OLIVER WOLCOTT, SECRETARY OF THE TREASURY.

A WAR COULD START AT ANY TIME. WE NEED 40,000 **MUSKETS** AS SOON AS POSSIBLE!

A **GUNSMITH** CAN MAKE ONLY A FEW MUSKETS IN A YEAR. BUT I HAVE A BETTER WAY.

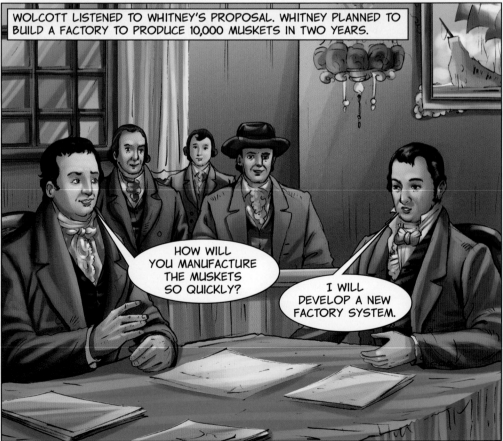

WOLCOTT LISTENED TO WHITNEY'S PROPOSAL. WHITNEY PLANNED TO BUILD A FACTORY TO PRODUCE 10,000 MUSKETS IN TWO YEARS.

HOW WILL YOU MANUFACTURE THE MUSKETS SO QUICKLY?

I WILL DEVELOP A NEW FACTORY SYSTEM.

IN THE 1700S, SKILLED CRAFTSMEN MADE MUSKETS. A CRAFTSMAN WOULD MAKE EACH PART, AND EACH PART WAS **UNIQUE**. THE PROCESS WAS SLOW.

WHITNEY WAS DETERMINED TO IMPROVE THE FACTORY SYTSTEM BY MAKING INTERCHANGEABLE MUSKET PARTS, ONES THAT COULD BE USED IN ANY MUSKET. THIS WOULD MAKE ASSEMBLY QUICKER AND SIMPLER.

OTHERS HAVE TRIED THIS, BUT WE WILL DO IT BETTER.

WHITNEY BUILT A NEW FACTORY IN NEW HAVEN, CONNECTICUT. THEN HE HIRED AND TRAINED EMPLOYEES.

I WILL LIVE ALONGSIDE MY WORKERS. THIS PLACE WILL BE CALLED WHITNEYVILLE.

IN 1799, WHITNEY WAS NOT EVEN CLOSE TO PRODUCING HIS FIRST ORDER OF MUSKETS. HE MET WITH SECRETARY WOLCOTT TO EXPLAIN.

ELI, YOU HAVE FALLEN BEHIND.

IT IS TAKING LONGER THAN I THOUGHT TO DEVELOP MY SYSTEM OF INTERCHANGEABLE PARTS.

SOME PEOPLE IN THE GOVERNMENT HAVE NO FAITH IN OUR NEW FACTORY SYSTEM. OUR CONTRACT COULD BE IN TROUBLE.

GO TO WASHINGTON AND SHOW THE SYSTEM TO THEM.

YES, THAT'S WHAT I'LL DO!

THIS IS A BETTER WAY TO BUILD A MUSKET. MY SYSTEM WILL MAKE REPAIRS IN THE FIELD EASY.

YES, I NOW SEE THE ADVANTAGES.

WHITNEY DEMONSTRATED HOW A MUSKET PART COULD FIT ANY MUSKET. HE WON OVER THE GOVERNMENT OFFICIALS TO HIS SYSTEM.

WHITNEY FINALLY FULFILLED HIS GOVERNMENT CONTRACT, THOUGH IT TOOK 10 YEARS. IN 1812, HE GOT ANOTHER CONTRACT TO PROVIDE 15,000 MUSKETS.

OUR SYSTEM IS FINALLY WORKING.

THAT MEANS OTHER MANUFACTURERS WILL USE IT.

EVERY MAN HAD JUST A FEW SIMPLE THINGS TO DO BY HAND OR BY MACHINE ON EACH MUSKET PART.

OUR MUSKETS ARE NOW FAST AND EASY TO MAKE.

IN 1812, WHITNEY APPLIED TO CONGRESS TO RENEW HIS PATENT FOR THE COTTON GIN.

THINK OF THE BENEFITS OF THE COTTON GIN. I HAVE RECEIVED VERY LITTLE MONEY FOR THIS GREAT INVENTION!

MANY MEMBERS OF CONGRESS HAD GROWN RICH FROM WHITNEY'S INVENTION. HOWEVER, THEY DECIDED AGAINST THE PATENT RENEWAL.

THE PEOPLE BACK HOME DON'T WANT TO PAY A FEE TO WHITNEY TO GIN THEIR COTTON!

WHITNEY MARRIED HENRIETTA EDWARDS IN 1817 WHEN HE WAS 51 YEARS OLD. THEY HAD FOUR CHILDREN.

WHITNEY DIED OF AN ILLNESS IN 1825 AT THE AGE OF 59. ALWAYS THE INVENTOR, HE MADE SEVERAL DEVICES TO RELIEVE THE PAIN OF THAT ILLNESS.

IN THE 1840S, ELI WHITNEY'S SON WOULD MODERNIZE AND IMPROVE THE FACTORY. HE FOUND NEW MARKETS FOR THE COMPANY'S PRODUCTS.

I WILL CARRY ON MY FATHER'S **LEGACY.** WE WILL MODERNIZE THIS BUSINESS.

THE ASSEMBLY LINE IDEA WOULD DEVELOP AND CHANGE. IN 1913, THE FORD MOTOR COMPANY DEVELOPED ONE OF THE FIRST MOVING ASSEMBLY LINES.

THE ASSEMBLY LINE THAT WHITNEY HELPED DEVELOP CHANGED THE WORLD.

# Timeline

| | |
|---|---|
| **December 8, 1765** | Eli Whitney is born in Westborough, Massachusetts. |
| 1775 | The American Revolution begins. |
| 1777 | Eli Whitney's mother dies. |
| 1779 | Eli Whitney's father marries Judith Hazeldon. |
| 1785 | Whitney begins attending Leicester Academy. |
| 1789 | Whitney starts at Yale College, in New Haven, Connecticut. |
| 1792 | Whitney graduates from Yale College. He travels to Savannah, Georgia, to start a tutoring position. Instead, he invents the cotton gin. |
| 1793 | Whitney applies for a patent on the cotton gin. |
| 1794 | Whitney and Phineas Miller sign partnership papers, starting the company Miller & Whitney. |
| 1795 | Fire destroys the main building of the Miller & Whitney factory. |
| 1798 | Whitney contracts with the US government to build 10,000 muskets in two years. |
| 1808 | Whitney completes the government order for 10,000 muskets. |
| 1812 | Whitney receives a second government contract for 15,000 muskets. |
| 1817 | Whitney marries Henrietta Edwards. |
| 1825 | Whitney dies at the age of 59. |
| 1841 | Eli Whitney Jr. takes control of the Whitney Armory. |

# Glossary

**American Revolution** (uh-MER-uh-ken reh-vuh-LOO-shun)  Battles that soldiers from the colonies fought against Britain for freedom, from 1775 to 1783.

**assembly-line** (uh-SEM-blee-lyn)  A system of workers and machines designed to mass produce products.

**Civil War** (SIH-vul WOR)  The war fought between the Northern and the Southern states of America from 1861 to 1865.

**cotton gin** (KO-tun JIN)  A machine designed to remove seeds from cotton fibers. It was invented by Eli Whitney in the 1790s.

**duplicate** (DOO-plih-kayt)  To copy or reproduce.

**economy** (ih-KAH-nuh-mee)  The way in which a country or a business oversees its goods and services.

**factory system** (FAK-tuh-ree SIS-tem)  A way of producing products in a factory.

**ginning** (JIN-ing)  Removing seeds from cotton with a cotton gin.

**green-seed cotton** (GREEN-seed KO-tun)  A type of cotton that could be grown in the upland areas of the South.

**gunsmith** (GUN-smith)  A person whose trade involves the making or repairing of firearms.

**interchangeable parts** (in-ter-CHAYN-jeh-bel PAHRTS)  Parts made to fit any manufactured item of the same type.

**legacy** (LEH-guh-see)  Something that has been handed down from another person or something left behind by a person's actions.

**manufacturing** (man-yuh-FAK-cher-ing)  Making something by hand or with a machine.

**muskets** (MUS-kits)  Long-barreled firearms used by soldiers before the invention of the rifle.

**patent** (PA-tent)  To get a document that stops people from copying an invention.

**plantation** (plan-TAY-shun)  A very large farm where crops are grown.

**textile mills** (TEK-styl MILZ)  Factories where cloth is made.

**trespass** (TRES-pus)  To take over the rights or possessions of another.

**unique** (yoo-NEEK)  One of a kind.

# Index

# Websites

Due to the changing nature of Internet links, PowerKids Press has developed an online list of websites related to the subject of this book. This site is updated regularly. Please use this link to access the list:

www.powerkidslinks.com/jgai/whit/